Recounting the Beat

The Miraculous Journey
of a Transplant Recipient

Camilla Jenal

Recounting the Beat

Copyright © 2020 Camilla Jenal

Published by Disruptive Publishing

> 17 Spencer Avenue
> Deception Bay QLD 4508
> Australia
> www.disruptivepublishing.com.au

Edited by Snowflake Productions

All Rights Reserved. No part of this publication may be reproduced, distributed or transmitted in any form, or by any means, including photocopying, recording, or any other electronic methods, without the prior written permission of the publishers. Brief quotations that are credited to the publication and the author are permitted.

Although some of the stories within this book pertain to matters of health, they are for information purposes only, and it is not intended that they replace medical advice in any way. The author and publisher will assume no responsibility for any actions resulting from the use of this book.

ISBNs:
For print: #978-0-6450274-8-8
For eBook: #978-0-6450274-0-2

Dedicated to my beautiful mother
and my generous donor

without neither of whom
I would be here to tell this story today.

On the 25th of November 2012, I was gifted a new heart.

This heart has enabled me to celebrate these extra years with my loved ones.

I'm writing this book for three main reasons:

The first, to enable my family and friends to comprehend how the journey felt from my side, and to realise how their love pulled me through.

The second, to provide hope to other patients currently waiting on precious organ donations.

And the third, perhaps most importantly, is to give my heartfelt thanks to my selfless donor family, and to all donor families who have ultimately given us recipients the greatest gift of all...

Life.

Recounting the Beat

The Miraculous Journey of a Transplant Recipient

Lounging in a Samoan resort by the crystal-clear lagoon of Saletoga with my two beautiful daughters beside me, it is hard to feel anything other than blessed for the second chance at life, which my heart transplant gave me seven years ago.

Kirsty, Camilla and Heidi, recently in Samoa, celebrating 7 years

Each and every day since I was gifted my new heart has not been taken for granted. But it is the rare and special moments like today that truly take my breath away and remind me of how wonderful life is.

Rewind to seven and a half years ago, when the medical team were faced with solemnly informing my family that there was no hope for me, and that my life support was to be turned off as my failing organs were too weak to undergo any operation. I went from knocking at death's door, to the cardiac surgeon buying me time by implanting a LVAD, to receiving a full heart transplant. It has been such a marvellous transition from the priest and family on bedside vigil on those dark and dismal days to the bright and happy life I'm now enjoying to the fullest. It still stops me dead in my tracks whenever my thoughts revisit the start of my journey.

Many experts say that after a life-changing experience such as an organ transplant, life becomes more precious and one doesn't sweat the small stuff, so to speak. I, for one, totally agree. My life has definitely become more precious and I appreciate it more than I ever did. I feel that my patience has deepened. My empathy has skyrocketed. Don't get me wrong, I'm no saint, and I still get pissed off from time to time. Usually it's caused by silly events that

I consider unworthy of being emotive. But I endeavour to let these feelings go as hastily as they arrive and not waste my energy on things that, in the big scheme, are totally trivial. At the end of the day there will always be moments, people, and behaviours that will upset us. But it's about how quickly we can release them without allowing it to envelop us with its toxicity. That is where the real power lies, and it's a power I try to practice consistently.

I remain in awe of the hidden strength I somehow dug deep enough to find that, together with my enormous will to live and the very power of love itself, brought me back to life even after the medical team had begrudgingly given up. They had nothing to offer me, and were reluctantly turning off my life support, preparing my family for their final goodbyes.

I can't help but wonder sometimes why my life was spared. Was it because my children still needed me? Was it because my aging mother, whom I now care for, would soon become my destined dependent? Or was I just lucky at the neediest time of my life? Whatever the reason for allowing me to continue living, I certainly appreciate it. And my major plan is to stick around for a while yet.

My story is filled with broken pieces, terrible choices and ugly truths. It's also filled with a major comeback, peace in my soul, and a grace that saved my life.

Attitude to Inspiration

Now, let me escort you back in time to 2001. A time which, in parts, is still somewhat of a blur to me, even though the enormity of the situation I was faced with is just as raw and intensely emotional as it was in its genesis.

After giving birth to my youngest child, Heidi, little sister to Kirsty, then aged six, I was at my happiest place in life. I believed my life was complete, and a bright future was mine to enjoy. My deck of cards was fully stacked. I was happily married at the time, and my two incredibly loving stepchildren had grown into fine young adults. I lived in a lovely rural area with my dogs and my children and many friends. Yep. Life was dealing me a royal flush, and I was overjoyed. Little did I know that my perfect world was about to fall apart on a slow path toward ultimate destruction which would culminate into a lengthy stay in ICU, pounding at death's door.

A few months after Heidi was born, I noticed a strange mark on my shin. Although its origination puzzled me, my concerns weren't huge. It wasn't until the following year, when a large mass appeared in my right breast, that I sought any kind of medical advice. A lumpectomy was performed on my breast at the local hospital, but even though the tissue was biopsied, the experts were baffled about its origin. I was referred to Wesley Breast

Clinic in Brisbane and, after much consultation and more pathology, a sketchy diagnosis of probable sarcoid was given. I immediately began researching this auto-immune disease and discovered that, although it is relatively common, very little is actually known about it, and it's ultimately incurable.

Still, even after knowing the facts, I was nonchalant and went about raising my children and enjoying my life in my perfect world. My diagnosis and consequent treatment were way out of my GP's scope of knowledge, so I was again referred to Brisbane, this time to the Princess Alexandra Hospital. Dutifully, I reported annually for four years to the immunology clinic for blood and lung function tests.

A few months later, I was demolishing an old, weathered, wooden garden shed with my sister-in-law when she noticed that the right side of my face had suddenly swollen up. I raced inside and checked my reflection, starting to panic. I quickly saw my GP, who referred me on yet again – this time to an oral maxillofacial surgeon on the Gold Coast. After lengthily scrutinising my face, the surgeon proceeded to biopsy the lump in my jaw, which to this day remains one of the most painful operations I've ever had. The pathology results again declared sarcoid to be the culprit. I was given prednisone, 10mg daily, to reduce the inflammation. And although the drug made me sick to my stomach, it worked, and the swelling subsided.

Even though the sarcoid had reared its ugly head on my shin, breast and face so far, my lungs – where sarcoid usually manifests – remained clear. My eyes were also fortunately spared the cruel hand of the disease.

However, fast forward to 2006 when I started to notice that I was often experiencing shortness of breath. I took my concerns to my GP, who sent me off for an echocardiogram to check my heart, and they found it to be enlarged and slightly sluggish. It was then that I added a cardiologist to my already long list of specialist appointments, which earnt me the title of "cash cow" by my husband, as none of these appointments were cheap!

Although I was overwhelmed, I still had no idea that my big heart would one day become so large that it would struggle to pump at all. I became a biannual patient at the Prince Charles Hospital's heart failure clinic in 2008, and tried a myriad of medications to hopefully assist my heart in beating stronger and delay the damage. It was at this point that a defibrillator was implanted in case my heart stopped completely and needed to be shocked back into rhythm.

Although I wasn't able to exercise as much as I would have liked, as I would find myself out of breath quite quickly, I soon adapted to my life limits and managed to enjoy my family life and hold down my nursing job. At every appointment, I was told that my cardiac function was declining until it stabilized at around 30% functionality, which my body surprisingly adapted well to.

I travelled to Bali alone in late May 2012, as my friend Lisa was there ahead of me and I wanted to join her for a week of relaxation. At Brisbane Airport, where I was departing from, I had to walk from the carpark to the terminal and I really struggled with my breathing. It was only at that moment that I truly realised that I wasn't actually as well as I'd believed. Still, I soldiered on. Although a moped (or bemo) then had to be my main form of transport in Bali due to this realisation, I had a wonderful holiday and many laughs there with my friend.

Camilla, Kathy and Lisa

Fast forward to the long weekend in June, which is now remembered as the Apocalypse rather than the celebratory tradition of the Queen's birthday, which is a luxuriating long weekend for many Australians. My brother Tim was living in Brisbane, and his partner Deb had her parents over for a visit from the UK. Charlie (my now-ex-husband) and I were invited up for lunch, which was actually incredibly lucky as it placed me in the vicinity of the only hospital capable of saving my life that day – the Prince Charles.

It was a four hour round trip and I wasn't feeling in top form that day, so we left soon after we ate. On the way home, I grew concerned as my breathing was becoming more and more laboured. I asked Charlie if we could quickly stop by the hospital. I remember apologizing at the counter of the ED clinic, insisting that it was probably nothing to be concerned about but I just needed my breathing assessed. And if they were too busy, I was happy to go on my way.

Well, 30 minutes later I was told that I had crashed, my organs were failing; my lengthy hospital stay had begun. I cannot remember much about the visit at all after that.

It still riddles me with guilt that whilst I was in hospital, I was oblivious to the fact that my family were emotional wrecks, frantically grouping together, taking time off work, and rushing to be at my bedside. I was later told the waiting room in ICU had never been so busy, as my closest friends and family took turns in coming and showing their love and support for me as I lay there motionless, and at times lifeless, while the medical team scurried around inserting tubes, doing scans and anything else they could to make my palliative stay more comfortable.

It was very soon realised that being placed on life support was the only option left to prolong my life long enough for everyone to be able to say their goodbyes. Three times during these dark days my family were given the grim news that I wouldn't make it through the night and they should come and see me one last time.

I am told that God must have grown sick of hearing my name as my Christian friends prayed, begged and did secret deals with him to spare my life. I am sure that this love played a major part in my improvement, along with my strong will to live, as the medical team stated that there is no medical reason why I managed to stay alive; they had no option but to cease all care, and yet are amazed that I continued to hang on after my life support was turned off.

They also proclaimed that my heart was the largest they had ever observed. It now sits in a science lab and is hopefully being put to good use for student cardiologists.

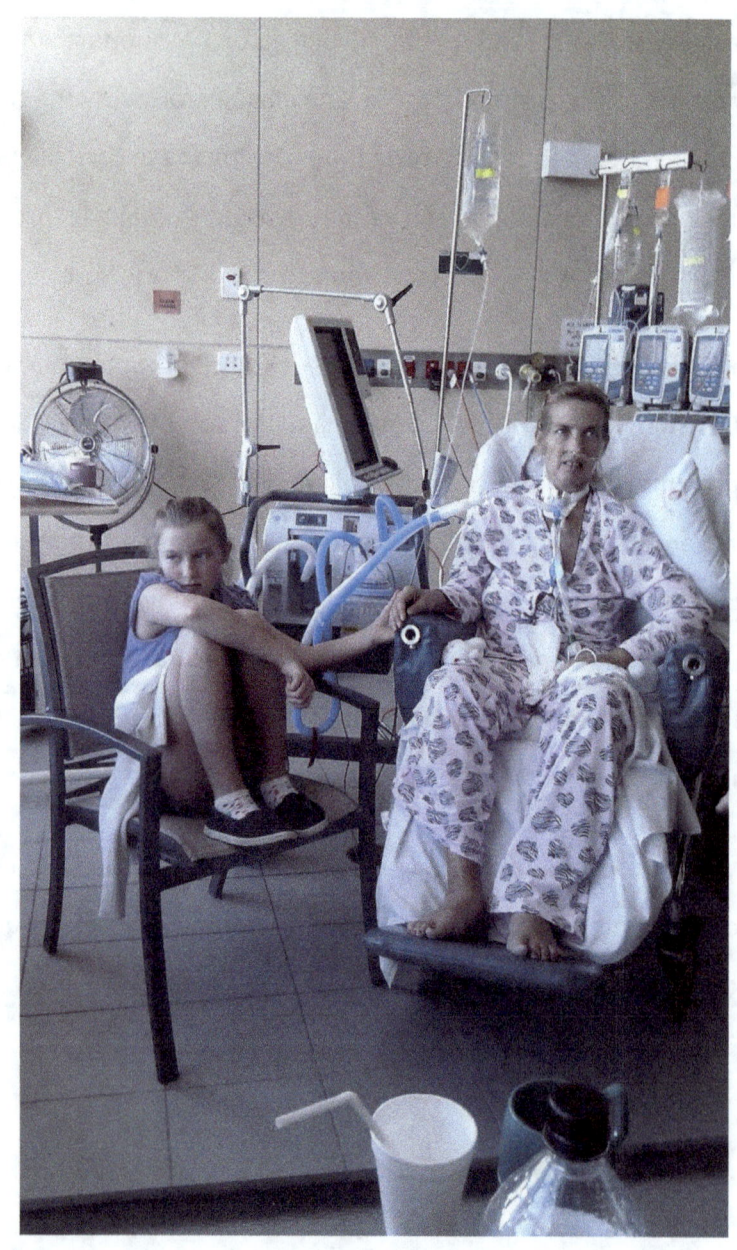

Heidi's 11th Birthday

Heidi's 16th Birthday

My brother's home became a revolving door with family flying up to stay, and shifts for visiting were put into place. My dear Mum spent most of her time praying in the church chapel and asking God to take her in place of me.

The family: Rosemary, Tim, Mum, Camilla and Melissa

Thankfully, that negotiation never had to be made, and my mother is still very much alive at the ripe old age of 95.

The night the medical team determined that there was no treatment that they hadn't tried and they would need to take me off the life support is a vague memory for me, but remains vivid and heartbreaking for my loved ones.

The priest arrived; I could hear and feel my family gathered closely around the bedside, and was expecting an imminent "TIME OF DEATH" announcement as I received my dying last rites.

My beautiful mum tightly held my hand in hers, never more keenly aware of how precious time is for families, and knowing that my husband had already indicated that the transplant team could retrieve in death whichever organs had the potential to save others from such agony.

My treating doctor reluctantly turned off my life support and told the family that he expected me to die within a couple of hours. He was amazed that I was still desperately clinging to life as the night ticked by.

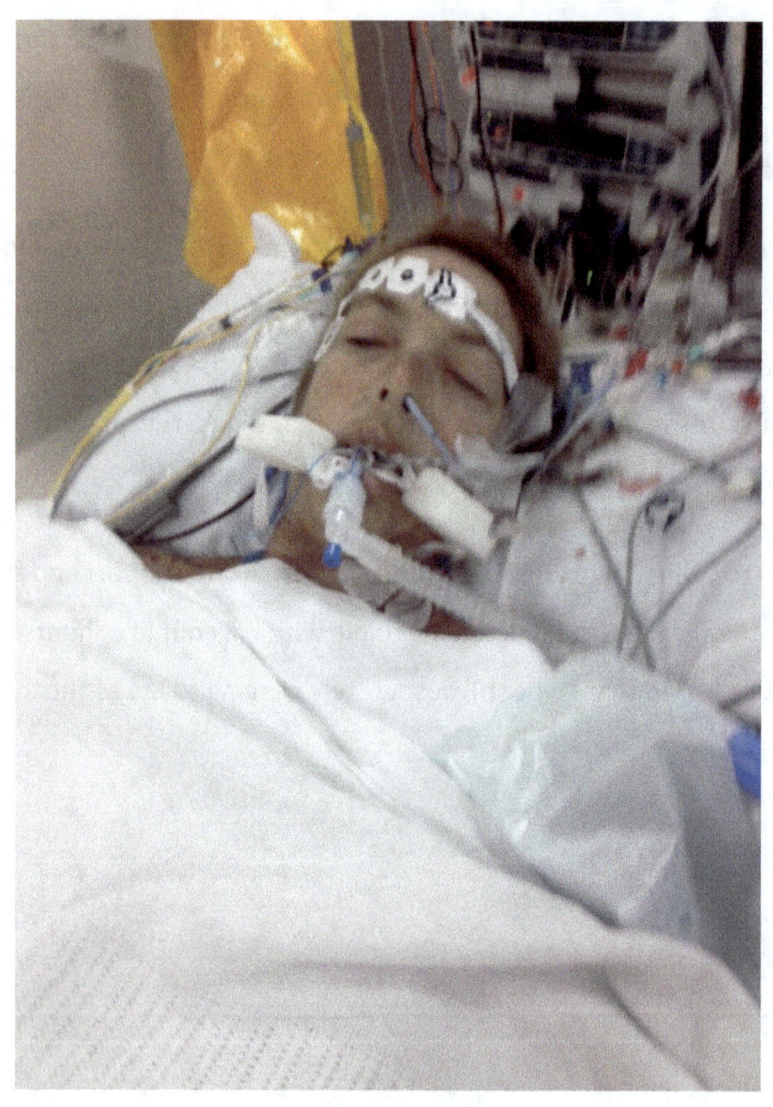

Camilla in a coma

At 1am I was still holding on. Some of the family were eventually convinced to go get some rest under the premise that they would receive a phone call if my condition changed . Apparently, my sister Melissa woke at 5am, convinced that she must have given her number incorrectly as her phone still had not rung. She grabbed mum and headed back to the hospital where she was met by the medical team, who were in shock as I had, by some unexplained miracle, survived the night so far, and my heart continued to beat.

I remember vaguely when I woke from the coma and mouthed to the bedside doctor, "how many days till Heidi's birthday?" as I knew it must be soon. She answered me, "8 days." With that, I looked into her eyes and pleaded, "keep me alive until then."

That was my motivation to keep fighting, as I did not want to ruin her birthday; after all, she and the rest of my family had suffered while I slept. Well, that wish was granted, and as the medical team did not think I had much time left, they allowed us to have a small birthday gathering complete with balloons and streamers on the balcony of the ICU.

Birthday party on the balcony of the ICU

All I wanted to do was be able to wish my daughter a Happy Birthday, and so, with the secret help of my speech therapist, a speaker was sought and placed over my tracheostomy for just long enough to say the words. Unfortunately, as I was only able to whisper and had to compete with all the background beeps of my life saving machines, my first, climactic words, which I had doggedly practised repeatedly, were muffled and unheard by my family. Frustratingly, I mustered all my strength and breath, and managed to ask the crowd for attention, and then repeated myself. An eruption of tears and cheers followed as everyone could hear me then.

Due to the superpowers of the poppy, I also experienced some wild and vivid dreams in my comatose state. One particular dream made for a very turbulent and emotional reality on awakening; when I aroused and saw the helium balloon beside my bed, I was convinced it was because I had a baby boy while sleeping. I demanded that the staff bring me my baby, and when they informed me that I had not given birth, I burst into tears. In my mind, I had produced a beautiful son.

Also, I was absolutely positive the cleverly disguised medication trolley was actually a mouth-watering buffet of exotic and tropical fruits, which I begged my visitors to bring me. Apparently, when my oldest and dearest best friend Kathy arrived, I asked her to go get me an icy cold beer; being the good friend that she was, she set off to find me one. Makes me laugh now, as I have no idea how I planned on getting it down my NG Tube, but I am sure I was dead serious at the time!!!

Since the day of Heidi's 11th birthday, I have been blessed to partake in many more birthdays and celebrate each and every one of mine and my loved ones'. I now also have an extra day to celebrate annually ... the anniversary of my heart transplant, a celebration of the greatest gift I have ever received.

The following day, July 3rd 2012, I received my LVAD, and within a couple of weeks I made it out of intensive care and into the cardiac failure ward.

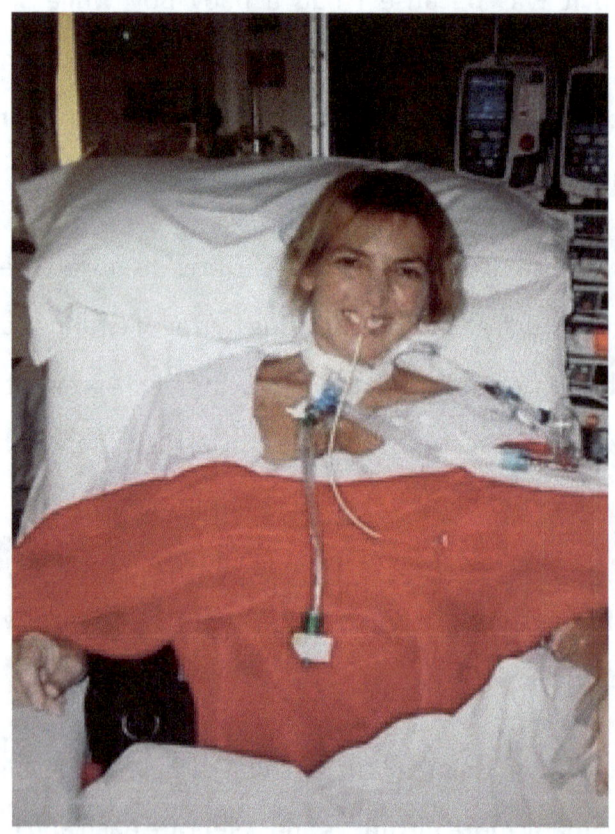

I'm alive!

My stoic children were my absolute rocks throughout my time in Ward 1B. Amazingly, Kirsty somehow managed to achieve outstanding academic results at school; as I write this, she is about to embark on a physio career after completing her masters at Griffith University. Needless to say, my heart bursts with pride.

My youngest daughter, Heidi, is also killing it; she's waiting to hear which university she will be attending this year to study veterinary science.

These girls, along with my stepchildren Ricky, and Alisha who with her husband Tony and their four children, are all to be congratulated on their resilience, and admired for the compassion, love and support which they showed during my illness and lengthy hospital stay.

Those long, boring drives and hospital visits must've been so tedious for my family, especially my young grandchildren. But I never heard a word of complaint and was always greeted with their infectious smiles and sloppy kisses.

Let me share with you some of the difficulties I experienced and events that occurred during my hospital stay leading up to my transplant. The saying goes that every day spent in the ICU takes at least a week to recover from. So, my 10 days in a coma called for a recovery period of over two months; the four total weeks calculated to a roughly a six-month rehab plan.

Here I must give credit to my support team. The care I received at the Prince Charles Hospital was truly sensational. The surgeons (whom we now refer to and claim as our national treasures), the heart failure team, the doctors, nurses and allied health assistants all went above and beyond their duties to provide us, the patients, not only with excellent medical care, but also the faith, hope and empathy to alleviate our fears and cling to life when at many times we felt like quitting. Being stuck in a hospital ward is not the most pleasant place to be, and at times was overwhelmingly scary and sad. But everyone from the cleaner to the CEO all tried so hard to make the best of that immense and depressing situation for me.

Thank you.

I can't even try to count the amount of times I have said those two words over the past eight years. At times I wish we had another way of expressing our gratitude, but every time I say thank you, I know it is coming from a place deep in my heart; I am reassured that although the words may be overused, they are never insincere. Especially not when you have been given a second chance and a rebirth like I and the rest of the transplant community have.

During my coma I'd had a tracheostomy inserted, which, although very necessary at the time, absolutely frustrated me when I tried to converse with my family and friends who had to try so hard to decipher my garble. I had a nasogastric tube for feeding, which brought with it a horrible feeding regime and a bitter metallic taste to my necessary supplements. As I improved, I forced myself to swallow the nauseating food so that I could gain the strength to commence my physio routine and start walking the path to get out of hospital.

After being taken off the life support and clawing my way back to the living world, I started doing physio – a regime I detested and loved simultaneously. At first, I could only walk a few weak steps before becoming extremely short of breath and drenched in perspiration.

While at times the exercise had me breathless, sweaty, trembling and full of tears, I obstinately persevered and ticked off many mini milestones along the way, which had the family and I break out into a celebration.

The day I was able to go to the toilet independently was probably my finest moment. It was a simple task that I will never take for granted again. And at times when I flush that loo, I reminisce and rejoice and do my happy dance, a private celebration of all that I have achieved.

Thank you.

Camilla on the mend

In case you aren't familiar with the marvellous piece of lifesaving equipment that is a Left Ventricle Assist Device (LVAD), it is a battery-operated mechanical pump used for end-stage heart failure patients which assists the left ventricle – the main pumping chamber of the heart – pump blood to the rest of the body. It does this using an impeller that spins thousands of times per minute.

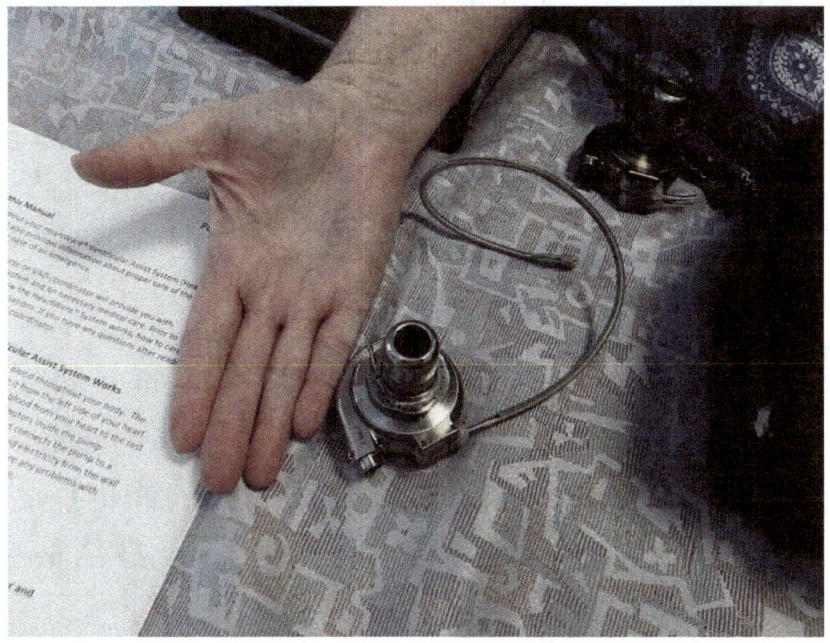

Photo of an LVAD, with an adult male hand for size

This made for a very interesting party trick with mates as while on the LVAD the patient has no pulse or measurable blood pressure. The patient's blood must remain very thin to prevent blood clots, so warfarin is added to your mega bucket of medications. There is also a huge risk for infection and bleeding.

An LVAD implant operation is typically an open-heart procedure and usually takes between four to six hours. As I was literally dying of cardiac arrests prior to my surgery, it started a heated debate among the surgeons about whether or not to even go ahead with it, as my chances of surviving the operation itself were extremely low. Even as I was being wheeled into theatre my heart stopped, and I clearly remember waking up to one of the doctors pounding on my chest.

I feel that at this point I must share with you that I'm no longer scared of death. Every time my heart stopped, I floated off into a most peaceful state and seriously considered staying there. I even recall being a little annoyed when the doctor woke me up from my heavenly slumber.

Of course, nowadays, I'm eternally grateful they insisted on bringing me back!

As miraculous as this lifesaving equipment is, the time spent living with one is not without its complications and inconveniences. Being battery operated means it could fail at any given time, without any notice. Therefore, a spare battery pack has to be within arm's reach of the LVAD recipient at all times.

This means that I had to have a trained minder to accompany me wherever I went. The minder had to ensure that they would be competently able to hook me up to the spare battery immediately if my original one failed. The hospital allows you to choose four carers to be trained, and so a rotating roster was formed, and Charlie and my friends selflessly rose to the task.

Kirsty, Tony, Angela, Anthony, Andeson, Camilla, Amanda, Alisha and Ally

Although I cannot express my gratitude enough for the love and support shown, at times it all became very invasive and claustrophobic, as I was not allowed to be on my own.

Luckily, we never had a complete battery fail during that time, although it did present some other challenges along the way. it turned out that the LVAD I was hooked up to was a newer, smaller, more modern aid which the medical staff were not wholly familiar with and were very inquisitive about.

I recall finally arriving on the ward when I was medically stable enough to be transferred from intensive care; my room had a flowing congregation of nurses, doctors and allied health assistants crowding around me with great interest. And although mine was not the first of its kind, I was the first patient on the ward to be a LVAD recipient of this newer model as the first recipient of this innovative LVAD had received her heart transplant while still in ICU. Occasionally It would emit a deafening alarm, which would have nurses and doctors scurrying to my bedside with very concerned expressions until it subsided without too much intervention.

I ended up becoming quite fond of my LVAD – so much so that I named him "Mervyn". I figured he was my new best friend, as we were literally joined just north of my hip! Mervyn was my saviour, as after having him implanted I gradually improved until finally, on July 30th, I was approved for and put on the waitlist to receive a heart transplant. I was ecstatic, as this meant that I was finally in hospital for a good, valid reason (I didn't consider rehab strong enough). I hoped a donor heart would be found quickly so that I could go home and be reunited with my family. My excitement was short lived; in early August the medical team discovered that

I had a kidney infection, which meant more surgery – and worse, they would have to take my name off the waitlist until they had operated. Fortunately, I made it back onto the list a few weeks later.

Having an LVAD means that you are not allowed to bathe, swim or in any way submerge the LVAD, as water is its worst enemy. Even having a shower was a precarious juggle, as the LVAD had to be bagged and taped to remain totally dry. As it was embedded into my body and had to be very close to me, dislodging this life support tube would have a drastic outcome. We all tried desperately hard to practice caution; however, one day, the moisture from the shower steam somehow managed to penetrate Mervyn, which caused a major complication.

As Mervyn was still so novel for the existing medical staff, the team ended up flying in a technician from England who had more experience with it. He took me straight to the surgical theatre while he swiftly turned off and dried the pump. My native heart, thankfully, managed to kick in with the adrenaline on board – just enough so for the experts to do their thing, dry my battery and then replace it. I was able to return to the ward, where I would wait for my donor heart to be allocated … or so I'd planned.

Not long after theatre, I noticed the pressure bandage they had applied to my left arm was becoming increasingly tight. I called the nurses, who initially stated to me that the bandage had to stay on to stop the bleeding, but once they saw my arm swelling uncontrollably, they quickly cut it off.

The pain was excruciating and didn't dissipate after the bandage was removed. I was literally writhing on the floor at this stage, and my hand was white and cold. Morphine was administered to ease my pain and fear. Apparently, my arterial line had tissued when they removed the cannula, and the compression of nerves caused a temporary block of perfusion to my hand. It was definitely the most painful time of my stay and beat my 35-hour childbirth labour pains hand down!

Another obstacle which presented itself throughout my stay was that Mervyn seemed to be alarming way too frequently and no one knew why, so after a while I was ordered to stop physio, take no showers and have no mobile phone communication. For me this was hugely depressing, as even though showers were difficult enough, those three activities were my cherished coping mechanisms to get me through this distressing time locked up within the four stark walls of my hospital room.

The long chain of sleepless nights became all too familiar. At times, my mind went through numerous thought processes jumbled around like jelly on a plate; feelings of anticipation and excitement about my donor heart becoming available, to a deep, hollow sadness at realising another precious life would be lost just to preserve mine. Those lonely nights were at times unbearable, and I dreamt of being able to go home to wait it out instead.

I was allowed, eventually, to spend time at home. However, living in NSW and being stuck in QLD brought with it a unique struggle between the border medical teams, as in the case that something drastic happened to me at home I needed the ambulance to take me back to QLD, which I found out was actually a huge hurdle.

I tried not to be depressed about not seeing my family, but I must admit my mental health was declining, and I desperately tried convincing the team to let me leave. I only now realise that they were also trying to set me free, but due to the restrictions imposed on dividing states, they couldn't. They were doing their best, however, and for that I am grateful.

Jane, my lovely nurse, was especially persistent in trying to keep my spirits up. She even took me out to a hairdresser one day, which was ultimately divine. She also managed to get me a gate pass to stay at my brother's place, and the motel near the hospital, which were a lovely and welcomed treat.

I was also allowed to visit the local shopping centre with my carer for an hour or two, which was very much appreciated. I remember one day when Charlie and I caught a taxi to the shops. Hopping out, excited for some retail therapy, we suddenly realised that the very important spare battery had been left in the taxi. Immediately we set off on foot to chase it, and lucky for us were able to find the cab and retrieve it before anything drastic occurred!

We never told the team back at the hospital as it may have meant no more gate passes, which were my greatly appreciated little escapes from hospital because otherwise, from the confinements of our ward, my ward buddies and I became bystanders to the outside world.

I distinctively recall watching the hospital gardeners on their routine grass mowing and yearning to smell the scent of freshly cut grass. Watching the rain fall also cruelly teased my senses, and

I tried hard to imagine the delicious aroma which emitted with the drenching soak.

I spent lots of time on my iPad listening to music, and when I would look at ocean themes, I would try hard to evoke the memories of the sounds of crashing waves and the smell of the salty sea breeze as it brushed my hair out of my face.

My window overlooked the hospital car park, and as I watched my family and friends depart the hospital grounds after a visit, I often cried myself to sleep, desperately longing for the day that I would be able to accompany them as they left.

"Never underestimate the power of a sloppy kiss and a wet nose on a bad day."

Ward 1B was a very hectic ward with a myriad of patients, all with one huge bond – that of a failing heart and dying to live, longing to be free, to be reunited with our families.

While I watched the newcomers arrive in the ward from the ICU, I also sadly watched a few of my ward buddies leave this earth, running out of time before a suitable transplant was found.

We experienced a rollercoaster of emotions as we all waited together. We were so alone in our quest for a second chance at life. We were an odd mismatch of patients, too, with so many differences – age, size, race, religion. But looking back, we shared such an unbreakable bond while we were all desperately trying to hang on to life long enough to receive the precious gift that a transplant could give.

A beautiful young 20-year-old girl was one of the first patients I met. Amanda had been struck down with acute cardiomyopathy after contracting the flu. I was absolutely devastated for her; one moment she was enjoying life to its fullest, as 20-year-olds do so well, and the next she was being hooked up to a pump, waiting for a transplant – her only chance of survival. It gutted me.

She did this with amazing grace, and warmly welcomed me to the hospital herd for waiting hearts. I am delighted to tell you that she did eventually receive that gift and made it home just in time to celebrate her 21st birthday.

Nowadays, a few years on, she is married and has defied the odds yet again by giving birth to two beautiful children. Such a courageous young girl, whom I've been blessed to stay in touch with; I thoroughly enjoy hearing about her miraculous and courageous journey post-transplant.

I eventually did make that triumphant return home on the 1st of November, after many tears and a lot of begging. I still had my LVAD but was ecstatic to be home and able to attend Kirsty's year-12 formal. She looked absolutely stunning, and my heart burst with pride.

Kirsty's year 12 formal

I also had the privilege of being able to indulge, attending my youngest daughter's completion of primary school celebration.

Life seemed to remain quite calm at home, and a new type of normal developed. A roster of minders was set up and seemed to be working ok, I was happy and became quite resigned to the fact that I would be spending Christmas at home with Mervyn by my side.

That was until the phone rang at 1:30am on the night of November 25th.

"Hi Camilla! How soon could you get to Prince Charles Hospital? It is still early, but we may have a heart for you!"

I tried to remain calm, but the adrenaline was already setting in; I raced around in circles. The girls woke and rushed into my room, breaking out laughing as I grabbed an assortment of odd shoes to pack. Eventually I got it together, and I said my goodbyes as Charlie and I began the long drive to Brisbane.

We didn't say much that trip. I think we were both desperately clinging to the hope that this was to be the gift to aid my failing heart. Once there, we were quickly escorted to my room and began filling in the forms; and so began the wait for the surgery theatre.

The next thing I remember is waking up and feeling extremely sore, and very nauseated. When the nurse came to me, I said that we had better let Charlie know the procedure didn't go ahead. She looked at me with tears welling and told me that the transplant had indeed gone ahead, and all was well.

I just cried and cried; I was so relieved. Apparently, I had a bleed post operation and was taken back to theatre, but they managed to stop it and I was going to be ok.

The next few days were a blur, mostly spent dozing on and off. My poor sister Ro flew up from Sydney to see me, and I spent her whole visit sleeping. Still, she forgave me, as did all my other visitors, as we were just so thrilled that my gift had been received, and life was wonderful once more.

Along the journey I have made so many lifelong friends who, like myself, would not be here without the gift. It is so special to have these friends who can totally understand the pros and cons of living with a transplanted organ.

Some of us have fared better than others, but we've all been hit with a trade off in some way or another, and many of us experienced firsthand some of the nastier side effects from our daily medications and our immuno-compromised bodies such as cancer, diabetes and kidney failure. We all support each other, however, and have formed a strong bond through sharing and off-loading our experiences, both the triumphs and setbacks.

As my health and fitness improved, I got back into my beloved sport of tennis and headed back to the gym. I also began to learn table tennis and dancing.

I have also competed at The Transplant Games, both domestically in Melbourne in 2014 and Gold Coast 2018, and internationally, as I was fortunate enough to compete in Malaga, Spain, for the World Games in 2017, winning Gold for Australia with my daughter beside me to cheer me on!

Camilla with her table tennis partner, Maria.

Camilla with Kylie at Donate Life Remembrance Day which is held annually Australia wide at different venues to honour our donor families

The Games are a lovely way of uniting all who have been touched by organ donation – including recipients, donor families and those waiting for a transplant. As well as being a great networking event and a lot of fun, the games also promote awareness of organ donation and demonstrate the living proof of how it can change, and ultimately save, many lives.

Camilla in the zone at the games

Camilla and doubles partner Linda receiving Gold at the 2017 World Games

The journal in which I wrote my thoughts on my time in the ward has been a treasured keepsake, and is quite cathartic, as it allows me to reflect when the need arises. When I felt well enough, I also asked for permission to read my progress notes, which they agreed to as long as a nurse was in attendance when I did so, as they were incredibly confronting.

I sometimes find myself struggling to fill the massive void of memories of the five long months that I spent confined to Ward 1B at Prince Charles Hospital. It is all so disjointed and foggy. For whichever reason, either the drugs, the anaesthetic or the trauma itself, I cannot fully recollect the missing pieces. Now, though, I'm content to let it go and be thankful that I'm making the very most of my second chance at life. For the most part I'm no longer struggling, preferring to be more in the present of the here and now. Being well enough to return to my nursing career has allowed me to give back some of the love and empathy I have received, and it absolutely thrills me to be able to do so.

Although usually a heart is donated from a deceased donor, there are cases where a living donor who is in need of a heart and lungs can donate their native heart onto a dying recipient in what is called the Domino Effect. Domino transplantation is very rare, and in the past 25 years only around 30 of these transplants have been performed Australia wide.

Currently in Australia, legislation mandates anonymity of deceased organ donation, although by using social media, many donors and recipients have found each other and established contact. During my lengthy hospital stay, I firmly believe in my heart that I crossed paths with the beautiful soul who ultimately became my miracle donor. My heroic angel keeps a watchful eye on me and keeps me safe.

I've written to my donor family and sent cards of my progress, including a teddy bear with a recording of my heartbeat, which I was told through Donate Life that they were thrilled to receive.

I would be honoured to have the pleasure of meeting them one day, and to answer any questions they may have. Or to simply hug and thank them. It would be my ultimate dream come true.

Looking back, I don't know why or how I got through spending so much time in the hospital without entirely losing myself. I do know, however, that the love and support from all those around me kept me going. The hope, even when at times I found my optimism waning, is the reason my heart beats today.

> There are more than 70 documented cases of transplant patients experiencing the same thoughts and feelings as their organ donors did in life. People have reported everything from craving the donor's favorite foods, to inheriting their talents. It's posed a theory that the cells in our body can store memories.
>
> überfacts

Without the organ donor, there is no story, no hope, no transplant. But when there is an organ donor, life springs from death, sorrow turns to hope, and a terrible loss becomes a gift."

- UNOS -

Camilla with her girls

Camilla enjoying her daughter's graduation

Camilla enjoying a meal with her mum and her girls

Camilla living life to the fullest

"When I'm gone and no longer around
When you've buried my body deep in the ground
I hope you've listened to what I have said
My organs are really no use when I'm dead.

Take them all out
Share them around,
Shout from the rooftops
A donor we've found!
My liver, my kidneys my lungs and my heart
Just a few things to give someone a start

S.Todd

www.ingramcontent.com/pod-product-compliance
Lightning Source LLC
Chambersburg PA
CBHW071415290426
44108CB00014B/1833